YOU CHOOSE BOOKS

EARLY AMERICAN BATTLES

AT THE BATTLE OF ANTIETAM

AN INTERACTIVE BATTLEFIELD ADVENTURE

D0067605

by Matt Doeden

Consultant:
Richard Bell, PhD
Associate Professor of History
University of Maryland, College Park

CAPSTONE PRESS
a capstone imprint

J
CHOOSE
3/18
31.99

You Choose Books are published by Capstone Press,
1710 Roe Crest Drive, North Mankato, Minnesota 56003
www.mycapstone.com

Library of Congress Cataloging-in-Publication Data
Library of Congress Cataloging-in-Publication data is available on the Library of
Congress website.

978-1-5435-0288-6 (library binding)
978-1-5435-0292-3 (paperback)
978-1-5435-0296-1 (eBook PDF)

Editorial Credits
Adrian Vigliano, editor; Bobbie Nuytten, designer;
Kelli Lageson, media researcher; Kathy McColley, production specialist

Photo Credits
Alamy: The Print Collector, 10; Bridgeman Images: Chicago History Museum,
USA, 77, Private Collection/Troiani, Don (b.1949), Cover, 67; Getty Images:
Fotosearch, 94; Library of Congress Prints and Photographs Division: 14, 20, 31,
36, 40, 47, 53, 57, 60, 69, 72, 100; National Archives and Records Administration:
83, 89, 98, 103; New York Public Library: Miriam and Ira D. Wallach Division of
Art, Prints and Photographs: 27; North Wind Picture Archives: 6; Shutterstock:
Alexey Pushkin, Design Element, Atlantis Images, Design Element, Lukasz Szwaj,
Design Element

Printed in the United States of America.
010830S18

WITHDRAWN

Table of Contents

About Your Adventure 5

Chapter 1
Forces Massing................................. 7

Chapter 2
Scouting the Enemy...................... 11

Chapter 3
Battle in the Cornfield 41

Chapter 4
Care in the Chaos.......................... 73

Chapter 5
The Battle of Antietam 101

Timeline... 106
Other Paths to Explore 108
Read More 109
Internet Sites 109
Glossary 110
Bibliography...111
Index..112

ABOUT YOUR ADVENTURE

You are on the front lines of the bloodiest war ever fought on American soil. The Civil War rages on as Robert. E. Lee's Confederate troops converge on the Union force led by George McClellan. Battle erupts near the small Antietam Creek, near Sharpsburg, Maryland. Can you survive the coming battle?

In this book you'll explore how the choices people made meant the difference between life and death. The events you'll experience happened to real people.

Chapter One sets the scene. Then you choose which path to read. Follow the directions at the bottom of each page. The choices you make will change your outcome. After you finish your path, go back and read the others for new perspectives and more adventures.

YOU CHOOSE the path
you take through history.

CHAPTER 1

FORCES MASSING

Smoke rises above the army camp. It hangs in the air like a thick cloud. The smell of it seeps into your skin and your lungs. But after a year on the front lines, the smell of smoke is welcome. The other smells that linger about camp are far less pleasant. Men are gathered by the thousands, and most haven't bathed in weeks.

An officer rides by on horseback. The horse's hooves leave deep prints in the muddy ground. Somewhere near the edge of the camp, the men stir. You can hear their hooting and hollering. That can only mean one thing. Battle is nearly upon you.

Turn the page.

You look out at the landscape around you. It's beautiful. Farms and rolling hills give way to dense pockets of forest. Not far from camp, the scenic Antietam Creek winds across the countryside.

The part of the war known as the Maryland Campaign is just starting to get into full swing. After a victory at Bull Run, General Robert E. Lee has directed his troops north. They have moved into Maryland, under the command of General Thomas "Stonewall" Jackson. Union General George B. McClellan has responded. And now, the two forces are on a collision course.

This peaceful-looking landscape is about to be the site of some of the war's deadliest fighting. And you'll be in the thick of it.

You wipe your brow and march to your post.

Whatever comes, you'll be ready.

To ride as a Union scout gathering intelligence on the Confederate forces, turn to page 11.

To fight as a Confederate soldier in the battle, turn to page 41.

To serve as a nurse in a Union field hospital, turn to page 73.

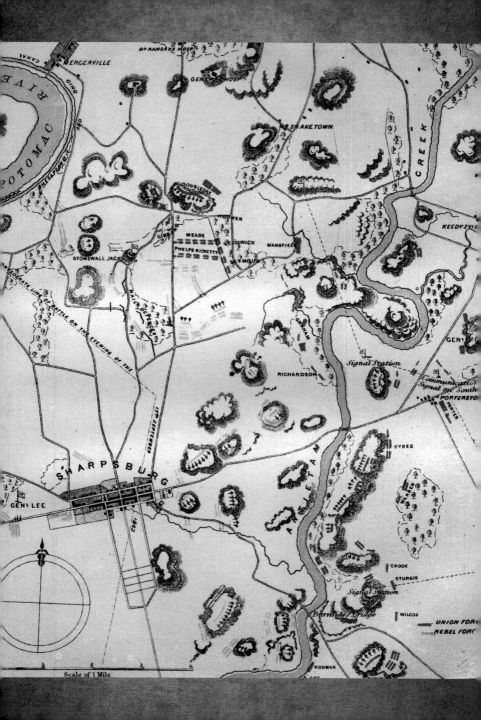

CHAPTER 2

SCOUTING THE ENEMY

"At ease, captain," barks your commanding officer, Major General Joseph Hooker. He walks quickly into the small building being used as the camp's command center. You relax your body but remain standing as he leads you to a small table set in the center of the room. The table is lit by several lanterns. On it lies a large map of Maryland.

Hooker is a tall man with dark, wavy hair. His saber rattles at his side as he moves around the table. Hooker points his index finger at a spot on the map. It's Antietam Creek.

Turn the page.

"The rebels are there, on the north banks of the creek, south of Sharpsburg," he barks. "We need to know how many there are and how many cannons they have. And we need to know whether they're mobilizing. You're one of our best scouts. Take a few men. Cross the river. Learn all you can and report back to me."

"Yes sir," you reply. Hooker sweeps out of the room as quickly as he arrived. You take another long look at the map, committing the image to memory. Then you step outside and gather your gear. Finally you summon two of your best men, George and Isaac, to join you.

"Just the three of us?" George asks. He's a private, a low-ranking soldier. But he grew up hunting and tracking animals and there's no one with better instincts in the field.

"It needs to be a small force," explains Isaac. He's a lieutenant and has one of the sharpest tactical minds you know. He can guess an army's size with just a look at its camp. He also understands better than you do exactly how both Union and Confederate commanders think.

The three of you collect your weapons and then mount horses. Your first task is to cross the Antietam Creek. The slow-moving creek winds through the countryside. You're on the southeast side of it, while the Confederates have camped along the northwest banks.

"There's a stone bridge to the south," George says. "That might be a good place to cross."

Isaac disagrees. "We're more likely to be spotted going that way. It's too close to the rebel camp. We could head north to cross, then double back under cover."

Turn the page.

General Joseph Hooker (1814–1879)

You scratch the scruffy beard that covers most of your face. You don't want to waste time by going north, only to double back. But walking into a Confederate trap doesn't sound very appealing either.

"What'll it be, sir?" Isaac asks.

To head south for the bridge, go to page 15.

To take the long route north, turn to page 17.

"To the bridge," you order. "There's no time to waste."

It's a short ride to where the stone bridge stands. The Antietam Creek flows slowly beneath it. In another time, this place would seem beautiful. But now, all you can see is the coming violence. Men will die here — lots of them. Maybe you will die too. A shiver runs down your spine.

"Wait here," George says as you approach the bridge. You and Isaac pull up while he rides slowly into a clearing. You watch as he scans the northern bank, searching for signs of the enemy. After a few moments, he brings his horse about and returns.

"Well, private," you say. "What do you see?"

Turn the page.

George shakes his head. "No sign of the enemy," he begins. "But it's too quiet. No birds, no animals. Something doesn't feel right."

Isaac scoffs. "No birds or animals? You can't be serious."

George looks at you. "I don't see any reason not to cross," he says. "I'm just saying that something seems odd here."

To turn around and head north, go to page 17.

To cross the bridge, turn to page 19.

The three of you set a brisk pace northward. The afternoon sun beats down on you as you ride along a wooded bluff. To the south and east, farmhouses dot the landscape. No one steps outside. The people here are afraid. So close to the Potomac River, which separates the North and South, their loyalties are torn. Many identify with the South, but Maryland stands with the Union.

The afternoon grows late as you finally reach a small wooden bridge, well north of your camp. The clip-clop of horses echoes loudly as you cross, but you're far north of the Confederate encampments. You cross without incident, then head south along the creek's eastern bank.

You ride into an open clearing. Suddenly, George stops. He throws up an arm, silently telling you to pull up as well.

Turn the page.

It takes you a moment, but then you see it. Two gray-uniformed figures stand across the clearing. For a moment, all five of you remain frozen in place. Then, in a whirl of motion, one of the Confederates raises his rifle and fires.

The shot misses its mark. Before you can respond, George has his rifle in hand. He's a brilliant marksman. He doesn't miss. His shot catches the Confederate shooter in the shoulder, spinning him around. Before either you or Isaac can shoot, the other officer flees into the dense woods.

"Rebels can't be far," Isaac says. "Those shots will have them coming, and soon."

To approach the wounded soldier, turn to page 21.

To leave him there and continue with your mission, turn to page 23.

"Thank you, private," you reply. "But we cross here."

You head into the clearing. George leads the way, while Isaac brings up the rear. The horses' hooves clop over the stone of the bridge.

When you're almost across, a loud shot rings out. George's horse rears up in surprise, and he crashes to the ground. Another shot follows. A puff of smoke rises from beyond the bluff directly ahead.

"Ambush!" Isaac shouts, wheeling about.

George's horse bolts across the bridge, sending George crashing down. He struggles to stand, clearly dazed by the fall. Another shot rings out. And another. A bullet hits the bridge just a few feet from you. It sends chips and dust flying into the air.

Turn the page.

Burnside's bridge in Antietam, Maryland

You haven't been hit yet, so these aren't Confederate sharpshooters. But you can't stay here. The shots will find their mark soon.

To rescue George, turn to page 25.

To run for it, turn to page 27.

George leads the way as the three of you approach carefully. The man is sprawled on the ground. Blood stains his uniform. His weapon lies on the ground — he's not a threat anymore. You ask the man for his name, but all he can do is grunt weakly in reply. He's conscious but in a great deal of pain. Judging from the wound in his shoulder, he's going to die without medical care.

"It's an officer, sir," Isaac observes.

"Well, that changes things," you reply. An officer makes a valuable prisoner. He might give up information about the enemy camp. But to take him prisoner would require you to abandon your mission.

"He'll die if we leave him here," Isaac says.

"That's not our problem," George replies. "He shot at us first."

Turn the page.

Isaac shakes his head. "It's war, private. You can't blame the man for fighting. But here and now, he's no threat. He needs care and he might have information."

"The battle will be long over before he talks," George argues.

Suddenly, a shot rings out. All three of you hit the ground. Your eyes scan the horizon. You think the shot came from a thick stand of trees to the north, but you can't be sure.

"Mount up!" you order.

To try to bring the wounded soldier with you, turn to page 30.

To flee without him, turn to page 33.

George starts to ride out into the clearing but you stop him. "Wait. We stick to the trees. Our mission hasn't changed. We need to bring General Hooker as much information as we can gather."

The afternoon sun begins to dip as you ride along the bluff overlooking the north bank of the creek. Smoke rises in the distance — a sure sign that the Confederate camp is near. You tie up your horses near the creek and continue on foot.

"Up there," George whispers, pointing to a rocky ridge. The three of you scramble to the top. The high ground allows you to see out over much of the landscape. The rebel camp sprawls out north of the creek. Dozens of cannons are lined up near a small white church.

"How many?" you ask.

Turn the page.

You can see Isaac's mind working. "I'd say 30,000. Maybe more. If I could get a better —"

Click.

You freeze in place. You know that sound. It's the hammer of a rifle being pulled back.

Slowly, you turn. Two gray-uniformed soldiers stand below you. You're staring straight down the barrels of their weapons.

To attack the soldiers, turn to page 35.

To surrender, turn to page 38.

"Private!" you shout, kicking your horse and surging ahead. In one fluid motion, you pull your horse up and grab George by the wrist. As you pull him up onto your horse's back, another shot rings out. Your horse whinnies and stumbles. It's been hit! The animal's back legs buckle, sending you crashing onto the bridge.

By the time you're on your feet, a dozen gray-uniformed soldiers stand before you. Each man has a weapon pointed in your direction.

"What have we here," says one of them. He's an older solider who you guess is a colonel. A gold tooth glimmers in the sunlight, and he speaks with a thick southern accent. "We seem to have captured an officer!'"

Turn the page.

Several of the Confederates step forward. They seize your weapons. They grab you and push you roughly toward the Confederate camp.

"I believe our generals will be eager to have a word with you," says the soldier. "And then you can have a nice stay in one of our finest prison camps. Who knows, you may even survive it."

THE END

To follow another path, turn to page 9.
To read the conclusion, turn to page 101.

George lies a few dozen feet in front of you. As enemy fire rains down on the bridge, you realize that you have almost no chance of saving him. So you wheel your horse about and ride for safety.

Nurses in a Union field hospital work quickly to help wounded soldiers.

Turn the page.

Another shot rings out. You are pushed forward in your saddle, as if someone just punched you in the back of the shoulder. Your horse gains speed as you realize that you've been shot.

"Come on, sir!" shouts Isaac from a stand of trees straight ahead.

You grow lightheaded as the blood pulses from your wound.

"Don't worry, I'll get you —" You black out before Isaac can finish his sentence. You don't expect to wake up again.

But you do wake up. You're in a Union field hospital. A nurse hovers over you, dabbing your shoulder with a rag.

You start to sit up but the nurse stops you. "You've lost a lot of blood," she explains. "If this shot had been just a few inches lower, you'd be dead right now. The surgeon isn't sure if you'll ever be able to use this arm again. I'm sorry. But it appears your war is over."

29

THE END

To follow another path, turn to page 9.
To read the conclusion, turn to page 101.

The Confederate officer groans as you haul him up onto your horse's back. Shots ring out as you mount up and flee. Your horse is battle-tested and sure-footed. Clods of dirt explode all around you as shots miss their mark. You zig and zag across the clearing until you're finally safe under the cover of trees.

"That wasn't wise, sir," Isaac says.

You shrug. "We'd been spotted. The mission was over. At least this way we've got something to show for it."

The three of you ride back to camp as quickly as you can. The Confederate officer has lost a lot of blood. He passes out well before you reach the bridge back to the south side of the creek. You ride directly for the camp's hospital, where nurses are busy preparing for the looming battle.

"Confederate prisoner!" you shout. "He has a rifle shot to the shoulder."

Nurses swarm around the man. They swiftly move him onto a stretcher, then a cot. They pull off his uniform to reveal the wound.

Dozens of soldiers lay wounded on the ground waiting for medical treatment.

Turn the page.

You back away as they call for a surgeon. "Will he make it, ma'am?" you ask one of the nurses. She is holding the man's bloody coat.

"We'll do all we can," she assures you. She flops the coat down on a nearby table. A small, off-white envelope falls out of one of the pockets.

You scoop up the envelope and look inside. Your jaw drops. The officer was carrying orders from General Stonewall Jackson himself! You smile and duck out of the tent. General Hooker is going to be very pleased with this information. You might even get a promotion out of it —

if you survive the battle, that is.

THE END

To follow another path, turn to page 9.
To read the conclusion, turn to page 101.

"Go!" you shout, bolting toward your horse. All three of you mount up as more shots sound from the stand of trees. Your battle-tested horse knows exactly what to do. It whirls about and sprints back across the clearing. George and Isaac are right on your tail. More shots ring out, but you safely make it to the cover of trees.

George's horse follows. Isaac, the least experienced rider, brings up the rear. He's only a few dozen feet from the trees when a shot catches him in the back. He spills off of his horse's back and crashes hard to the ground.

In a flash, you and George grab him and pull him back into cover.

You look down at Isaac. He's badly wounded. He's losing blood at an alarming rate. He looks up at you. His skin is already growing pale.

Turn the page.

"We'll get you help!" you promise as the two of you lift him onto George's horse.

"Go!" you shout. The two of you ride as fast as you can, back toward the Union camp. But Isaac is fading fast. You doubt that he'll make it.

Your mission is a failure. You haven't gathered any intelligence. And now you've lost a good soldier and a friend. You just hope that you can do something in tomorrow's battle to make up for your failure.

THE END

To follow another path, turn to page 9.
To read the conclusion, turn to page 101.

Without a moment's hesitation, you launch yourself at one of the men. He's so startled by your sudden movement that he doesn't fire his weapon. You tackle him, sending his rifle flying from his grasp. It skids away down the rocky incline.

Behind you, George opens fire. His shot catches the remaining Confederate soldier square in the chest. The man slumps to the ground without a sound. Meanwhile, Isaac has thrown himself on top of the Confederate you tackled. He pins the man down as you use a strip of cloth to bind his hands.

"Should we take him?" Isaac asks.

"No time," you reply. "A gunshot so close to camp is going to bring a lot of attention. Leave him. Let's go!"

Turn the page.

General Joseph Hooker (front, second from right) and his men in 1863.

You lead the charge down the rocky slope.
You sprint to your horses, untie them, and
mount up. It's a mad charge through the woods.
You can hear voices shouting behind you.

After several minutes of charging through
the brush, you allow your horses to slow their
pace. Your heart is racing and sweat drenches
your navy blue uniform. But you're safe.

"I wish we'd gotten a better view of their camp," Isaac says. "We might have been able to pinpoint some weak spots."

You nod. "True. But we know more now than we did when we left. The general will be glad for every detail we can give him. Hopefully, the intelligence we gained today will help us win the day tomorrow. The Union needs a victory and just maybe this will be it."

THE END

To follow another path, turn to page 9.
To read the conclusion, turn to page 101.

You drop your weapon and put your arms in the air. "We give up! Don't shoot!"

George looks at you with disgust, then drops his rifle. Isaac does as well. Both men look away, unwilling to make eye contact with you.

"Well, well," says one of the soldiers. He looks more like a boy than a man. A mop of brown hair hangs over his sweaty face. "A fresh batch of Yankees, just for us!"

The Southern soldiers march you at gunpoint into their camp. The men here look exhausted. But they also look eager. The war has been going well for the South, and they remain confident in their cause.

You are now a prisoner of war. You are bound by the wrists, interrogated, and beaten. And that's just a taste of your life to come. The war will drag on for years. Can you survive that long?

You don't like your chances.

THE END

To follow another path, turn to page 9.
To read the conclusion, turn to page 101.

CHAPTER 3

BATTLE IN THE CORNFIELD

"Mmm... salted pork again," says Abner, looking down at a small plate. "How nice."

You smile. Abner is a good soldier and your closest friend. But there's nothing he won't complain about.

You take a bite of the tough meat. It's true, you've grown awfully sick of salted pork. But at least it's food. With the war ramping up, the Confederacy has a lot of soldiers to support and limited resources to do it. You're grateful for any food you can get.

Turn the page.

You look out over the rolling countryside and at the large cornfield beyond your camp. The dawn sky is streaked with orange.

"I'll be happy to eat that for you if —"

BOOM! The rumble of cannon fire sends you both scrambling to your feet. "It's starting!" calls out another soldier. All around you men in gray Confederate uniforms begin to form ranks.

Abner stares blankly at his food. "Just my luck," he grumbles.

You chuckle as you reach for your rifle. "I thought you hated salted pork."

Abner just shrugs. "I do. But that doesn't mean I didn't want to eat it."

The sound of musket fire carries toward you as you rush to the front lines. Confusion reigns as the army braces for battle. "Where are they?" shouts one man.

Abner points. A Union flag flies above the cornfield. The corn itself moves, as if a great wave is washing through it. You realize that the wave is the enemy.

"Are you ready?" Abner asks.

"It doesn't look like I have a choice," you say.

To engage the Union troops at Miller's cornfield, turn to page 44.

To fall back to fight with an artillery unit near headquarters at a small church, turn to page 47.

You lie down, side-by-side with your unit, as the blue-uniformed Union troops burst out of the tall corn.

"Rise!" orders Colonel Marcellus Douglass. The long line of Confederate infantry rises as one and takes aim. "Fire!" shouts the colonel. You point your rifle at the mass of soldiers emerging from the corn stalks and pull the trigger. The sound of your shot is lost in the deafening rumble of battle. Not even knowing if you hit a target, you set to reloading.

The Union troops form ranks along the edge of the cornfield and return fire. A shot whizzes right past your ear, missing you by inches. To your left, a man you've known since the beginning of the war clutches at his gut and doubles over. All around you men are dying.

You raise your rifle and fire again. Neither side has any cover. At such close range, it's a slaughter on both lines. Dust and smoke hang thick in the air. Your ears ring from the constant sounds of gunfire.

"Yankees approaching from the pike!" Abner shouts, pointing behind you and to the west. A small dirt road, the Hagerstown Turnpike, is lined on each side by wooden fences. As the Union troops advance, part of the Confederate line breaks away to defend the pike.

Another shot zips close past you. You're not hit. But Abner's muffled grunt tells you that he is. You grab your friend as he slumps to the ground.

Turn the page.

Abner's left leg is soaked in blood. The wound doesn't look mortal — at least if he gets some treatment soon. But his face shows that he's in terrible pain.

"Let's go!" he groans. "I'll be fine. We have to defend the pike. We can't let the Union break the line."

To stay and try to stop the bleeding, turn to page 50.

To join the forces defending the Hagerstown Pike, turn to page 52.

Dunker's Church is a small, white building that stands on a low rise overlooking an open field. Rows of cannon are lined up outside the church. You and Abner quickly take your positions beside a cannon along the left edge of the line.

Dunker's Church near Antietam, Maryland

Turn the page.

"Look, it's General Jackson," Abner says, pointing toward the small church. Stonewall Jackson is a living legend among the Southern troops. You've seen him several times but have never met him. You hope to survive the battle and get that chance.

The boom of cannon fire pulls your attention back to the battle. "Union infantry approaching!" shouts an officer.

"They're moving to flank us," Abner says. "We can't let them get around our line or they can collapse in on us from both sides."

The battle erupts. You aim your cannon toward the cornfield, sending volleys into the Union troops advancing there. The ground shakes each time you fire the huge gun.

A Union shell explodes a short distance in front of you. "They're returning fire!" you shout.

Just then a mass of Union forces emerges from the trees. The soldiers are almost on top of you. All around you, men attach bayonets to their muskets and rifles, preparing for close combat.

To join in the ground fighting, turn to page 55.

To continue firing into the cornfield, turn to page 66.

There's no way you're leaving your best friend untreated on this field. You grab your knife and cut a long strip of cloth from Abner's trousers. Even as your fellow soldiers fall back, you remain on the field of battle.

The wound is in his lower thigh, so you wrap the cloth strip a few inches above it. "This is gong to hurt," you warn Abner as you twist the ends of the cloth to tighten the tourniquet. Abner shouts out in pain but you don't stop. You twist until you can't get it any tighter, then tie off the ends. Already the bleeding has slowed. Abner has passed out — probably from the pain. But you're confident that he'll live.

By the time you look up, your unit is gone. They've fallen back to defend the pike. A wave of Union blue swarms over the field. They are moving toward what remains of the Confederate line, which is advancing into the cornfield. It's only a matter of moments until they're upon you.

To dash for the line of Confederate troops, turn to page 57.

To lie down next to Abner and play dead, turn to page 59.

Abner grits his teeth and stands. You'll just have to hope that he won't lose too much blood.

The Union troops line up along the east side of the pike. You and Abner are among the Confederates who line up along the west side. Wooden fences on each side are all that separate the two armies.

Before the first shot is fired, Abner slumps to the ground, unable to stand. You and another soldier work quickly to create a tourniquet. It will have to do — the other soldiers are lining up in formation. Abner hobbles to his feet, and you both step into line.

You open fire. At such close range, the death toll is terrible. Soldiers on each side stand no more than a few dozen feet apart. In front of you, the wooden fence explodes as a round strikes it. It sends slivers of wood through the air.

Many men lay dead in a ditch after the bloody battle at Antietam.

"Union troops to the rear!" Abner shouts. You wheel about to see a chilling sight. You've been so focused on the enemy ahead that you never realized that more Union troops have flanked you. They are approaching from behind, through an area called the West Woods.

Turn the page.

"They're surrounding us!" Abner calls, terror creeping into his voice. He's right. You can't possibly fight the Yankees on both fronts.

"What do we do?" Abner asks.

To flee, turn to page 63.

To hold your position, turn to page 65.

The line of Confederates moves toward the Union troops. You grab your rifle, attach your long, curved bayonet to the end, and join in the charge.

The armies meet on an open field. The sounds of gunfire are replaced by the clash of bodies and blades. As you attack you're separated from Abner. You see him several dozen yards away, running into a sea of blue. You clash with a charging Union infantryman, sending him sprawling to the ground. You charge into the mass of men and bodies, slashing and bashing your way through.

Abner is only a few feet away when a Union soldier catches him. The Yankee stabs your friend with his bayonet. "No!" you shout, rushing to Abner's side. The surging battle moves on as you hold his head in your arms.

Turn the page.

"Tell my wife that I love her," Abner rasps.

You eye a group of trees, away from the fighting. A shot whizzes a few feet over your head. You've got to get Abner to cover.

"Tell her yourself," you answer, reaching under Abner's arms in an attempt to drag him.

Abner weakly bats your arm away. "No. I'm finished. Go."

To try to move Abner to safety, turn to page 68.

To say goodbye, turn to page 69.

You've done what you can. The battle still rages all around you. At such close range, and without any cover, this is a living nightmare. Only the constant roar of gunfire drowns out the moaning of the countless wounded.

Union and Confederate soldiers fought at close range at Antietam.

Turn the page.

You rise to join the largest group of Confederate troops you can see. It's not your unit, but at this point, it doesn't matter. You take off in a mad dash.

You're a single gray-clad soldier, exposed on this deadly field. You never have a chance. The moment Union sharpshooters spot you, they take aim. The first shot catches you in the arm. A second clips your calf and sends you sprawling to the ground. As you fall, the third shot strikes you in the chest. That's the shot that finally ends your war — and your life.

THE END

To follow another path, turn to page 9.
To read the conclusion, turn to page 101.

You look toward the Confederate line, then back toward the Union troops. You'll never make it. The moment you rise, a dozen rifles will be aimed directly at you. So you do the only thing that you can do. Your hands are covered in Abner's blood. So you smear it over your face and flop down on the dusty ground next to him.

For what seems like ages, you lie completely still. Eventually the sounds of battle recede. You can hear the distant roar of artillery and battle cries, as well as the groaning of wounded troops.

Slowly, you stand, looking out at the devastation around you. Bodies are everywhere. In the distance a mobile ambulance moves through the field. Nurses and field surgeons with the ambulance do their best to tend the wounded. But it's a Union unit, and you're not about to let your friend fall into enemy hands.

Turn the page.

Union officers and nurses from the U.S. Sanitary Commission in Fredericksburg, Virginia

Abner regains consciousness as you splash water from your canteen onto his face. His eyes are glassy and his gaze is distant but he seems to understand. You help him stand, supporting him so that he doesn't have to put any weight on his wounded leg.

Under the cover of the smoke and dust,
you make your way back toward headquarters.
Abner tires quickly, so you move slowly over
the next several hours. But you avoid the battle
itself. Before long, you're safely behind the
Confederate line.

"I can't go any farther," Abner huffs.
He's exhausted. The two of you slump down
along a rocky ridge. That's where you stay
until you hear the rumble of wagon wheels —
a mobile ambulance.

You breathe a sigh of relief when you realize
this one is Confederate. You wave the ambulance
down, and two nurses rush to Abner's side.

"Your friend will be all right," one of the
nurses tells you. "He's lucky. It's madness
out there. More dead and wounded than I
can count."

Turn the page.

"Who's winning?" you ask.

The nurse just shakes her head. "Nobody. Nobody is winning. Come, now. We'll help you rejoin your unit — however much of it remains."

THE END

To follow another path, turn to page 9.
To read the conclusion, turn to page 101.

It's madness all around you. Men are dropping their weapons and running — often straight toward the enemy. "We have to go!" you answer, grabbing Abner by the arm and pointing southwest. "The Yankees are coming at us from the north and the south. Maybe we can get around their line that way."

The confusion of battle works in your favor as you make your way toward the West Woods. A haze of smoke and dust helps you move out of harm's way. Abner leans on you for support as you head into the West Woods. You're now west of where the Union troops are advancing.

Turn the page.

Your battle isn't over, however. From your cover in the trees, you aim your rifles and fire volley after volley into the Union ranks. The battle soon spreads into the West Woods and you join a unit of Texans.

By the time the day is over, you can't believe all you've seen. The massacre at Miller's Cornfield. The fighting in the West Woods. Even the South's doomed counterattack to hold a critical stone bridge. Somehow, you and Abner survive the battle.

You're the lucky ones. Thousands of soldiers lose their lives at Antietam. The memory of the battle will haunt you for the rest of your days.

THE END

To follow another path, turn to page 9.
To read the conclusion, turn to page 101.

"Hold your ground!" you shout, firing again through the fence. You concentrate on firing and keeping as steady as possible. Abner props himself up against the fence and takes aim. You're amazed that he can still hit his targets despite favoring his left leg.

It's a brave stand. But it's also doomed. The Yankees press in from both sides. As you reload your rifle to shoot again, you feel something like a sharp punch to the chest. For a moment you don't realize what's happened. Then you feel it. The bullet has pierced your chest.

Blackness creeps in around the edges of your vision. Your knees buckle and you slump to the ground. You are just one of more than 22,000 casualties of the terrible Battle of Antietam.

THE END

To follow another path, turn to page 9.
To read the conclusion, turn to page 101.

"Keep firing!" you shout. You can't do anything about the advancing troops. But you can still do your part in driving back the Union forces advancing through the tall corn. You fire another shot. The shell rips through the corn. The corn is so tall and thick that you can't be sure what you've hit. You continue firing anyway.

BOOM! A cannon only a few dozen feet away explodes as a Union shell blasts into it. Debris flies through the air. A large jagged piece of metal pierces into your side. You can feel the red-hot metal bury itself deep inside your gut.

You slump to the ground. Abner, who somehow avoided being hit, cradles your head in his arms. The pain is unbearable. You open your mouth to speak, but you can't form the words. Abner just stares down at you, his eyes welling with tears.

Confederate General Longstreet watches over his men as they load a cannon.

Blackness closes in around your eyes as the life fades from your body. "Goodbye, my friend," Abner whispers. They're the last words you'll ever hear.

THE END

To follow another path, turn to page 9.
To read the conclusion, turn to page 101.

"No," you tell Abner. "I'm not losing you, not today." But even as you say the words, you see your friend's expression grow slack and his skin grow pale.

You pull him toward the trees as the battle rages on. Suddenly, you feel a strange tingling sensation in your chest. Your knees buckle and you slump to the ground, landing on top of your friend. You've been shot.

You can't breathe — the round has pierced your lung. With the last of your strength, you grab Abner's hand. You're sorry you won't be able to fulfill his final request. But at least you'll die with your best friend at your side.

THE END

To follow another path, turn to page 9.
To read the conclusion, turn to page 101.

Abner's complexion pales. His eyelids flutter. Your throat grows tight as the realization sinks in. Your best friend is dying. You take him by the hand. "Goodbye, my friend," you say with tears in your eyes.

The 14th Indiana Volunteers help wounded Confederate soldiers after the Battle of Antietam.

You're not sure if Abner can even hear you. You give him one last look, then rise to your feet and rejoin the battle.

You fight with a heavy heart. The battle drags on and on. You retreat, advance, and withdraw again. By the end of the day, little has changed. Neither side has won the battle and the ground is soaked in blood.

You sit in a daze as darkness falls over the Confederate camp. Someone places a hand on your shoulder. You look up. But you're in such a state of shock that you barely recognize General Jackson.

"I saw you out there, young man," he says. "You fought bravely."

You nod. As Jackson turns to move on, you stand.

"Was it worth it?" you ask.

Jackson gives you a long, tired look. "I don't know, son. I don't know."

Maybe it was worth it. Maybe someday you'll look back and understand. But right now, you know what your answer is. This slaughter is madness. And it won't be over for a very, very long time.

THE END

To follow another path, turn to page 9.
To read the conclusion, turn to page 101.

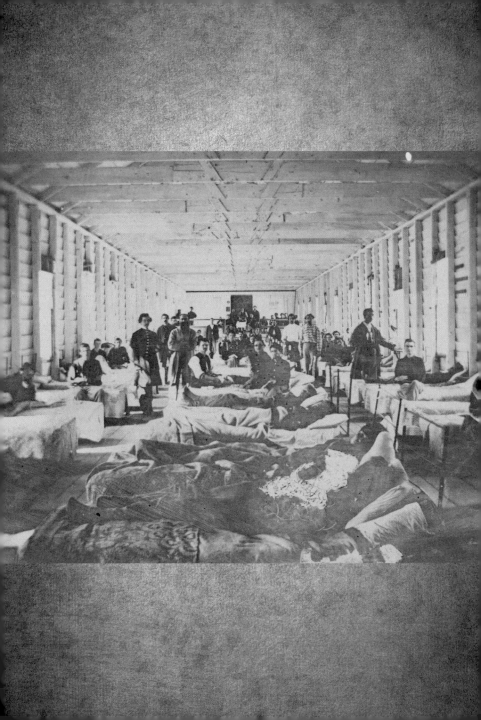

CHAPTER 4

CARE IN
THE CHAOS

It's not long after dawn that the wounded begin pouring in. Already, your nursing apron is splattered with blood.

In front of you, a man in a blue uniform screams in pain. "It burns! It burns!" You try to say something to soothe the man, but he can't hear you. The artillery explosion that left him burned has also left him nearly deaf.

On another cot, a Confederate soldier lies unconscious. His left leg has been amputated. This is how it goes inside the small field hospital just outside of Sharpsburg, Maryland.

Turn the page.

As far as you can see, there's pain, suffering, and death. Even as you struggle to treat patients and ease their pain, the roar of the ongoing battle never seems to end.

There will be more patients — lots more. You're just 20 years old, but already you've witnessed more death and suffering than anyone ever should. Out of nervous habit, you reach up to your hairnet. It holds your long dark hair in place. Whenever you get anxious, you find yourself checking it.

"Nurse!" shouts Holt, one of the surgeons. He's preparing to remove a musket ball from the shoulder of a young Confederate officer. Morphine is in short supply, so the man will be conscious during the painful procedure. You move to help Holt, but a fellow nurse, Sheila, is already by his side.

Outside, mobile ambulance teams gather. Many men are so badly wounded that they need care out in the field. Brave surgeons and nurses go out in these horse-drawn wagons to treat them.

"We need more nurses out here," shouts a voice. You look to Sheila. She had planned to go with the mobile team, but now she's busy assisting Holt. She's so focused on her patient that she doesn't even hear the call for nurses.

You've never joined one of the mobile teams. The idea of working so close to the actual fighting fills you with dread. And there are plenty of patients here who need care.

To take over for Sheila in the surgery, turn to page 76.

To volunteer for one of the mobile teams, turn to page 79.

You stride across the floor and gently touch Sheila's arm. She's placing a leather strap into the mouth of the Confederate so that he won't hurt himself during the surgery.

"They need you out on the field," you say softly, taking the leather strap and holding the soldier by the hand.

Sheila simply nods, touches you on the shoulder, and heads outside. You admire many of the nurses and surgeons at this makeshift hospital, but Sheila has become your mentor and hero. She never fails to put her patients first and doesn't even seem to notice which side they fought for. This war has made her a widow at age 35, yet she's the strongest woman you know.

A field surgeon's kit containing knives, blades, and other tools

Holt begins. The officer bites hard on the leather strap as the surgeon digs into his flesh. The man breaks out in a deep sweat, and his eyes roll back in his head as he loses consciousness.

After several grueling minutes, the surgeon removes the musket ball and sews the wound shut. "Bandage this patient and move on to the next," he orders you.

Turn the page.

You carefully wrap the patient's shoulder. As you do, the man slowly regains consciousness.

"The surgeon has removed the ball," you explain softly.

The man reaches for your hand. His breathing is rapid and shallow. He may be going into shock. The man tries to speak, but he's overcome by a fit of coughing.

"Nurse!" cries a nearby patient.

"Please help me!" begs another.

More patients are streaming into the hospital by the minute. Yet the young Confederate continues to cling to your hand.

To pull yourself free and attend to other patients, turn to page 81.

To remain with the young officer for a few moments more, turn to page 83.

You stand up straight, take a deep breath, and stride out of the field hospital. There, a surgeon is loading his gear onto a small horse-drawn ambulance. "Get on," he orders, then climbs onto the wagon himself.

You follow orders. Already on the wagon is a dark-haired woman who appears to be in her 40s. She wears a long gray dress with a white apron. It takes you a moment to realize who she is.

"Miss Barton?" you ask. You've heard of the famous Clara Barton, but you've never met her. She's a legend of the nursing corps for helping to gather much-needed medication, as well as for her work in the field.

"Call me Clara," she says with a nod.

Turn the page.

The wagon jolts as the driver sets off at a quick pace. "We're headed to Miller's Cornfield," he explains. "It's where the heaviest of the fighting was this morning."

You've seen the aftermath of other battles. But never anything like this. Bodies litter the ground. They're piled on top of each other along fences that run along either side of the road. And while the battle here has died down, it's not truly over. The sounds of nearby gunfire and booming still thunder over the land. As soon as the wagon stops, the surgeon hops off and starts to work on a wounded Union soldier. Barton is a step behind.

To strike out on your own, turn to page 86.

To go with Clara Barton, turn to page 87.

You gently pull away from the young man's grasp. "I'll check on you when I can," you promise. And then you're off. The wounded continue pouring in. The battle is a terrible one, and you're hopelessly understaffed.

You help perform three amputations. You clean the bedpans of soldiers inflicted with dysentery, an infection of the intestines. You bring soldiers water and what little medicine you have. It's only as dusk begins to fall that you remember the young Confederate officer and your promise.

He's not in the cot where you left him. Sheila, back from the field, tends to a patient several cots away. "What happened to the young officer with the shoulder wound?" you ask.

Turn the page.

Sheila doesn't look up. "The officer —
he tried to get up. He was in a panic. But with
all the blood he'd lost, he fainted and hit his
head. The surgeons tried to bring him back,
but he passed."

The news is a blow to your heart. You don't
know why. It doesn't make any sense. You've
lost countless patients before. Yet there was
something about him — a connection. You
suddenly feel very sad and overwhelmed.

You just don't want to do this anymore.

82

To resign your position in the nursing corps,
turn to page 91.

To continue caring for patients, turn to page 97.

This young man is scared and you can't bear to pull yourself away from him. You remain by his cot a few moments more. You squeeze his hand and whisper, "I have to tend to other patients now."

Clara Barton was a famous Civil War battlefield nurse. She went on to start the American Red Cross.

Turn the page.

The officer, calmer now, seems to understand. He lets go of your hand and closes his eyes.

The day stretches on. You lose track of how many patients you treat. You bring them water. You dole out what little medicine is available. You help as surgeons remove musket balls and amputate legs.

The wounded keep pouring in. It doesn't take long until the cots are all filled. You help lay the men on the floor, often having to step over them to move about the crowded field hospital.

"Help clean this up," another nurse calls to you sometime around dusk. A soldier with a severe case of dysentery lies on a soiled cot. Dysentery, an infection of the intestines, causes terrible diarrhea. It has struck this man severely.

You hold your breath and quickly gather up the soiled sheets. As you carry them away, you notice the young Confederate officer you treated before. He's sitting up on his cot but looking pale. "You shouldn't be up!" you shout to him, but he doesn't seem to hear you. It looks like he's going to stand up. With as much blood as he's lost, he's almost certain to faint.

To take the soiled bedding outside and clean up, turn to page 92.

To rush to the officer's aid, turn to page 95.

There's no time to waste. There are countless men here in desperate need of care. You move in the direction of the cornfield, quickly using what bandages you have. You help those you can help. You comfort those you cannot. And you call for the surgeon whenever you find a patient whose life depends on immediate care.

You feel so helpless. No matter how much you do, it seems to barely make a difference. Death is everywhere and you can't stop it. You begin to fall into despair. Tears flow down your cheeks. At one point, you collapse onto the ground and sob. You're not sure you can do it anymore.

To abandon your post and leave nursing behind you forever, turn to page 91.

To continue caring for patients, turn to page 97.

Clara seems unworried about the battle that still rages on nearby. Even as bullets whiz overhead, she moves from man to man, helping as best she can.

"Water, please," begs one soldier. He has a gunshot wound to his abdomen. You've worked in the field hospital long enough to know that he won't make it. Yet Barton kneels over the man, lifting his head and helping him sip some water.

Something zips past your ear. The sleeve of Barton's dress ruffles.

"A bullet hole!" you gasp. Sure enough, the sleeve of her dress now has a small hole in it. But your wonder over this doesn't last long. The bullet missed Barton by less than an inch. But it struck the soldier whose head she was cradling. The man lets out a grunt, then goes limp.

Turn the page.

It's heartbreaking. But you know that it's also a mercy. A shot to the gut is one of the most painful ways to die. The man may have held on for days in terrible pain. But with the state of medicine in the field hospitals, he had little chance to survive.

You remain by Barton's side. When you run out of bandages, you use corn husks to dress the wounds.

In time, you return to the field hospital. It's not until sundown that the fighting finally stops. But the wounded just keep coming. In the days that follow, there's not nearly enough staff to care for everyone. The dead lie in great piles along the road outside of the hospital.

The battle lasted just one day. But the devastation stretches for weeks. You do all you can but it doesn't seem like nearly enough. You watch fellow nurses and surgeons fall ill from the diseases they treat. Medicine grows ever more scarce, and infections tear through the hospital.

Fellow soldiers surround a fallen man who must have an amputation.

89

Turn the page.

Yet you continue to fight. The loss of each patient pains you, but there are also successes. In spite of it all, some men do recover and return to their lives. The odds are stacked against you, and them, but you'll never stop fighting.

THE END

To follow another path, turn to page 9.
To read the conclusion, turn to page 101.

You can't go on. You thought you could handle this, but you were wrong. Wiping tears from your face, you stand up and just start walking. As you move, you can hear the cries for help all around you. But you block them all out. "Those men will die no matter what I do," you tell yourself. "I'm helpless."

You head to Baltimore, to start your life over. But the horrors of war never really leave you. You wake up at night with cold sweats. You have nightmares that you can't quite remember in the morning.

You do your best to lead a normal life. But you feel like a hollow shell of your former self. Part of you died at that hospital, and try as you might, you can never quite get it back.

THE END

To follow another path, turn to page 9.
To read the conclusion, turn to page 101.

You're carrying a load of soiled bedding. You need to get it out of the hospital as quickly as possible. You shout again at the officer, "Lie down please," but you don't stop moving. You pile the bedding outside for cleaning, then scrub yourself down before returning to the hospital tent.

You find the young officer in his cot. Sheila, back from the field, hovers over him. "He fell and struck his head," she explains, pointing to a gash in the man's forehead. "Will you bandage this?"

You carefully wrap the man's head. "Thank you," he says with a hoarse voice. It's the first time he's been able to speak to you. "Thank you for everything."

You smile. "What is your name, sir?"

"Lieutenant Harper, 53rd Georgia Infantry," he answers.

The days stretch on. Thousands are dead and countless more are wounded. The conditions and overcrowding of the field hospital become almost unbearable. You lose some patients but also save many. Through it all you keep a close eye on Lieutenant Harper. The two of you talk in those rare moments that you're not busy tending other prisoners. He grows stronger by the day, and so does your friendship. One day when he's well enough, the head nurse clears him to be moved to a Union prison. You wish him farewell with tears in your eyes.

"Find me after all of this is over," he tells you, looking back over his shoulder.

Turn the page.

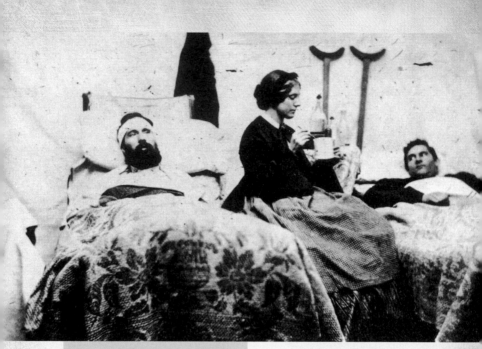

A nurse feeds soldiers in a Union field hospital.

You smile and nod. You hope you will see him again, one day. But until then, you'll do everything you can to save the victims of this terrible war.

THE END

To follow another path, turn to page 9.
To read the conclusion, turn to page 101.

The man is about to faint. Without a second thought, you drop the soiled bedding and rush to his side, just in time to prevent his fall. Dizzy and confused, he thanks you as you help him lie back down and place a cold cloth on his forehead. You don't even realize until later that in your hurry, your apron was exposed to the soiled bedding of the dysentery patient.

The next few days are very difficult. Wounded overflow from the hospital. The dead are piled outside along the road. The young officer — Lieutenant Harper — begins to recover, then suddenly falls ill.

A day later you feel the first symptoms of dysentery. They hit you very hard. Within two days you're too weak to stand. You can't even keep water down and slowly begin to dehydrate.

Turn the page.

On the third day, Sheila stands by your bedside with a sad look. "Lieutenant Harper passed this morning," she explains. But you're so delirious that the news barely makes sense.

The battle of Antietam created more than 22,000 casualties. You will never be counted among that number. But that doesn't change the fact that Antietam Creek was the site of your demise as well. You're buried in a small, unmarked grave. History will remember the brave nurses who served their countries in the terrible war. But your name won't appear in any history books. You will be lost to history, remembered only by those men whose lives you helped to save.

THE END

To follow another path, turn to page 9.
To read the conclusion, turn to page 101.

You want to leave and never return. You've seen so much suffering and death. It's draining you. It's making you feel numb inside.

You stop and take a deep breath. *No*, you tell yourself. *I'm not leaving. I'm needed here and I won't let my patients down.*

You vow to yourself that no matter what, you'll carry on as long as you can. And that's what you do. The days, weeks, and months all become a blur. As the war rages on, you're right there on the front lines, every step of the way. And no one breathes a deeper sigh of relief when it's all over than you do.

It's 1865. After four long and bloody years, the war is over. The North has prevailed. The slaves are free. "What's next?" Sheila asks you as the last of the field hospitals shuts down.

Turn the page.

President Lincoln visits the battlefield at Antietam in October 1862.

"Former slaves are moving north by the thousands," you answer. "Most are penniless. They've received little or no medical care all of their lives. I've been serving soldiers for so long. I think it's time I serve others. I am a nurse. I'll continue to be a nurse."

Shelia smiles and places a hand on your arm. "I like the sound of that," she says. "If you don't mind, I think I'll join you."

THE END

To follow another path, turn to page 9.
To read the conclusion, turn to page 101.

CHAPTER 5

THE BATTLE OF ANTIETAM

The Battle of Antietam was the bloodiest day of the Civil War — and of any war fought in the United States. There were more than 22,000 casualties in this one-day battle. The landscape around Antietam Creek was described as having turned red with blood.

The battle came at a pivotal point early in the war. Under the command of Robert E. Lee, Confederate forces had achieved a string of victories over the North. Looking to press his advantage, Lee marched his troops north into Union territory in early September 1862.

George B. McClellan, the Union commander, responded by trying to flank the Confederate troops. The two sides converged on the small Antietam Creek. The first shots were fired around dawn of September 17.

Union forces outnumbered the Confederates by almost two to one. But McClellan was cautious. He never committed all of his forces. Lee, meanwhile, threw everything he had into the battle. The fighting raged across Miller's Cornfield, along the Hagerstown Turnpike, and into an area called the West Woods. Over the course of one day, the back-and-forth fighting left both armies badly depleted.

Military historians believe that if McClellan had committed all of his troops, the Union would have been victorious at Antietam. Instead, the two sides fought to what is widely considered a draw.

Union General George McClellan (1826–1885)

The fighting did not resume on September 18. Both sides were badly hurt, and neither was willing to advance. That evening, Lee's forces began a retreat, which stretched on into September 19. Lee's men marched south, back across the Potomac River and back into Confederate territory.

The battle itself was considered a draw. But Lee's retreat gave President Abraham Lincoln the "victory" for which he had been waiting. Five days after the fighting, Lincoln issued his Preliminary Emancipation Proclamation — the final version was released on January 1, 1863. The proclamation ordered the end of slavery in the Confederate states. Southerners refused to follow Lincoln's orders. But the Emancipation Proclamation gave the North a strong new focus of fighting to end slavery.

Antietam was bloody and brutal. But it also marked a turning point in the war. Lee was forced to halt his advance northward. The draw robbed him of the momentum he had built. Instead of a swift victory, the South had to settle for a long and costly war. Had Lee won at Antietam, the South may have won the war. Instead, the better-equipped North wore down the Confederate forces, and Lee was forced to surrender three years later.

TIMELINE

April 12, 1861—The Civil War begins when Confederate forces fire on the Union-held Fort Sumter in Charleston Harbor, South Carolina

August 30, 1862—After three days of fighting, Confederate General Robert E. Lee's Army of Northern Virginia is victorious over Union General John Pope's Army of Virginia at the Second Battle of Bull Run

September 4, 1862—General Lee's Army of Northern Virginia enters Maryland. This was Lee's first invasion of the North during the Civil War

September 7, 1862—Union General George McClellan's Army of the Potomac pursues Lee's forces in Maryland. McClellan is cautious and careful to keep his army between the Confederates and Washington, D.C.

September 14, 1862—Union forces defeat the Confederates at the Battle of South Mountain, near Boonsboro, Maryland

September 15, 1862—Confederate forces defeat the Union at the Battle of Harpers Ferry, near the border between Maryland, Virginia, and West Virginia

September 17, 1862—The Battle of Antietam begins at dawn. Some of the most intense, close combat of the war occurs over the next 12 hours

September 18, 1862—Both armies are badly depleted. They each withdraw. In the evening General Lee orders the South's retreat

September 19, 1862—Lee's army crosses back over the Potomac, into Confederate territory

September 22, 1862—President Lincoln issues his Preliminary Emancipation Proclamation, ordering the end of slavery in the Confederate states

April 9, 1865—The Civil War effectively ends as Confederate General Robert E. Lee surrenders to Union General Ulysses S. Grant in Appomattox Court House, Virginia

OTHER PATHS TO EXPLORE

In this book, you've seen how events from the past look different from three points of view. Perspectives on history are as varied as the people who lived it. Seeing history from many points of view is an important part of understanding it. Here are ideas for other Civil War points of view to explore:

+ Field surgeons faced life-and-death decisions every day. They worked in poor conditions. Medicine was often in short supply. What would life be like as a field surgeon? How would you feel when one of your patients died? How could you keep your concentration when surrounded by so much death and suffering?

+ General McClellan did not commit all of his troops to the Battle of Antietam. Many historians believe that his caution allowed Lee's army to fight the Union to a draw. Why might McClellan have made that choice? How might the war have played out differently if McClellan hadn't held back some troops? Support your answers with examples from at least two other texts or valid Internet sources.

READ MORE

Burgan, Michael. *Spies of the Civil War: An Interactive Espionage Adventure*. North Mankato, Minn.: Capstone Press, 2015.

George, Enzo. *The Civil War*. New York: Cavendish Square Publishing, 2015.

Otfinoski, Steven. *Yankees and Rebels: Stories of U.S. Civil War Leaders*. North Mankato, Minn.: Capstone Press, 2015.

INTERNET SITES

Use FactHound to find Internet sites related to this book.

Visit *www.facthound.com*

Just type in 9781543502886 and go.

GLOSSARY

amputation (am-pyuh-TAY-shun)—the removal of an arm, leg, or other body part, usually because the part is damaged

artillery (ar-TIL-uh-ree)—cannons and other large guns used during battles

bayonet (BAY-uh-net)—a long metal blade attached to the end of a musket or rifle and used in hand-to-hand combat

casualties (KAZH-oo-uhl-tees)—people killed, wounded, or missing in a battle or in a war

Confederate (kuhn-FE-der-uht)—a person who supported the South during the Civil War

flank (FLANK)—to attack the far left or right side of a group of soldiers, a fort, or a naval fleet

infantry (IN-fuhn-tree)—a group of people in the military trained to fight on land

intelligence (in-TEL-uh-jenss)—information about an enemy's plans or actions

mission (MISH-uhn)—a military task

Union (YOON-yuhn)—the Northern states that fought against the Southern states in the Civil War

Yankee (YANG-kee)—a nickname for Union soldiers during the Civil War

BIBLIOGRAPHY

Alexander, Ted. *The Battle of Antietam: The Bloodiest Day.* Charleston, S.C.: History Press, 2011.

Keegan, John. *The American Civil War: A Military History.* New York: Vintage Books, 2010.

Schultz, Jane E. *Women at the Front: Hospital Workers in Civil War America.* Chapel Hill, N.C.: University of North Carolina Press, 2004.

Sears, Stephen W. *Landscape Turned Red: The Battle of Antietam.* New Haven, Conn.: Ticknor & Fields, 1983.

Ward, Geoffrey C., with Ric Burns and Ken Burns. *The Civil War: An Illustrated History.* New York: Knopf, 2009.

Weigley, Russell Frank. *A Great Civil War: A Military and Political History, 1861–1865.* Bloomington, Ind.: Indiana University Press, 2000.

INDEX

amputations, 73, 81, 84
Antietam Creek, 8, 11–12, 13, 15,
  101, 102
artillery, 12, 23, 47, 48, 66, 73

Barton, Clara, 79, 80, 87, 88
bayonets, 49, 55

Confederate Army, 13, 18, 23–24,
  25–26, 35, 41, 44, 45, 48, 51, 52,
  55, 58, 59, 61, 70, 73, 101, 102,
  104, 105, 106, 107

Douglass, Marcellus, 44
Dunker's Church, 23, 47, 48
dysentery, 81, 84, 95

Emancipation Proclamation, 104,
  107

field hospitals, 28–29, 30–32,
  73–74, 76–78, 81–82, 83–85, 88,
  89–90, 91, 92–93, 95–96, 97
Fort Sumter, 106

Grant, Ulysses S., 107

Hagerstown Turnpike, 45, 46, 51,
  52, 102
Hooker, Joseph, 11–12, 23, 32

intelligence, 12, 22, 23–24, 32, 37

Jackson, Thomas "Stonewall," 8, 32,
  48, 70–71

Lee, Robert E., 8, 101, 102, 104,
  105, 106, 107
Lincoln, Abraham, 104, 107

Maryland Campaign, 8
McClellan, George B., 8, 102, 103,
  106
Miller's Cornfield, 42, 43, 44, 48,
  51, 64, 66, 80, 86, 102
mobile ambulances, 59, 61, 75,
  79–80

nurses, 28–29, 30, 31, 59, 61, 62, 74,
  75, 76, 89, 96, 99

Potomac River, 17, 104, 107
prisoners, 21–22, 25–26, 30–31, 39

sharpshooters, 20, 58
slavery, 97, 99, 104, 107
surgeons, 59, 74, 75, 76, 77, 79, 80,
  84, 86, 89
surgeries, 76–78, 84

Union Army, 28–29, 43, 44, 45, 48,
  49, 51, 52, 53–54, 55, 58, 59, 63,
  64, 66, 73, 80, 101–102, 102, 104,
  105, 106, 107

West Woods, 53, 63, 64, 102